ANTON WEBERN

SYMPHONY

Op. 21

T0084321

Ernst Eulenburg Ltd

London · Mainz · Madrid · New York · Paris · Prague · Tokyo · Toronto · Zürich

CONTENTS

PREFACE

A symphony penned by Anton Webern (1883–1945), master of the small and smallest, the aphoristic form? Since the genre was established by, in particular, Haydn and Mozart during the period of Viennese classicism, didn't it after all continue to evolve – beginning with Beethoven – not only in terms of dimensions, but also in content? The Romantic symphony ultimately led from Schubert by way of Brahms, Bruckner, Berlioz, Sibelius or Shostakovich, to mention only a few exponents, to Gustav Mahler's monumental works: he experimented with extremes, shattering conventions involving duration, orchestral scoring, thematic construction, intensity and formal structure. Webern in his *opera*, on the other hand, radically reduced virtually all parameters: with, amongst others, minimalistic orchestration, brief playing duration, preference given to ranges of *piano* dynamics, transparent structure – and in thematic construction, with the realisation of the twelve-tone and serial-row techniques of the "Second Viennese School" (of Schoenberg, Berg, Webern). What a contrast from Gustav Mahler's eighth symphonic opus, the colossus of the *Sinfonie der Tausend* [Symphony of a Thousand] lasting nearly an hour and a half, to Webern's *Symphonie*, Op. 21, scored like chamber music, lasting less than ten minutes.

For Anton Webern, composer or conductor, the years from 1922 were alternately characterised by success and failure, always attended by financial problems: 'If only I could finally end up in an independent position, in order to be able to devote myself just to my work! […] What is more natural than that a composer is simply there to compose!',[1] appealed Webern to the publisher Emil Hertzka of the Viennese Universal Edition. And his urgent call for help prevailed: As of 1926, the publishing house

granted him a monthly allowance, later even to be increased. The same year, with the première of his *Fünf Stücke für Orchester* [Five Pieces for Orchestra], Op. 10, in Zurich at the *Internationale Gesellschaft für Neue Musik* (IGNM = International Society for New Music), he was able to achieve a success, spreading his name (as composer) far beyond his country's borders – a recognition that as conductor he had meanwhile already gained. As a creative mind, however, he still felt largely misunderstood.

In 1927 Webern composed his *Streichtrio* [String Trio], Op. 20 – the first instrumental work after nearly ten years of vocal works – and was probably already preoccupied with the idea of a symphony. This he then also concluded in August 1928, heading it in the engraver's model for the publishing house as: – *Symphonie für Klarinette, Baßklarinette, 2 Hörner, Harfe, 1. u. 2. Geige, Bratsche und Violoncell* [Symphony for Clarinet, Bass Clarinet, 2 Horns, Harp, 1st and 2nd Violins, Viola and Cello], *op. 21*, dedicated to "My daughter Christine", his third daughter, born in 1919. The première under Hermann Scherchen, already announced in the journal *Anbruch*, did not, though, come about – why is not clear. In June 1929, the American *League of Composers* announced the commission of a chamber-music work, with an honorarium of 350 dollars. A compromise was made in favour of the *Symphonie* – already completed –, which was then also premièred on 18 December, accompanied by riots that were, however, rather musico-politically based. Shortly thereafter, the composer conducted the work in Vienna on 24 February 1830; Otto Klemperer conducted it the following year in Berlin, and it was performed that same year at the IGNM festival in London. Webern's publishing house, the Universal Edition Vienna, already printed the score in 1929.

Arising from the late-tonality in Webern's works around 1899 were increasing tendencies

[1] Quoted from Wolfgang Martin Stroh: *Anton Webern. Symphonie op. 21* (= *Meisterwerke der Musik* 11) (Munich, 1975), 3. He offers the most detailed investigation of this work's musical structure.

IV

to expand harmony and expressivity, but also to use unusual colours, differentiated dynamics and articulation, combined with structural questions centred around variation and permutation techniques. The string-quartet compositions *Fünf Sätze* [Five Pieces], Op. 5 (1909), and *Sechs Bagatellen* [Six Bagatelles], Op. 9 (1911), were decisive stages – evidence of extreme stringency and, in the case of the *Bagatellen*, of the general departure of the Schoenberg pupils from the conventional tonality: The pieces are written virtually totally in the teacher's technique, thus in the 'composition with twelve tones related only to each other'. Ultimately, this then becomes the tendency as of the *Kinderstück* [Children's Piece] (1924, for piano, without opus number), and the *Drei Volkstexte[n]* [Three Traditional Poems], Op. 17 (1924, for voice and chamber ensemble). Emerging from Webern's construction of the row – divided into groups of six tones, in particular, and using old contrapuntal techniques (inversion, retrogression, retrograde inversion) – was 'an especially dense web of relationships'[2] – tonality was eliminated and the formal coherence superseded by a close motivic network.

Like the Op. 20 trio and the Op. 22 quartet, the symphony, Op. 21, was also initially conceived in three movements. After the first sketch for a third movement also in the symphony, Webern decided to leave it as a two-movement structure. The composer himself writes about the underlying row: 'The series reads: F-A flat-G-F sharp-B-A/E flat-E-C-C sharp-D-B. – It is idiosyncratic in that the second part is the retrograde of the first [...] thus here there are only 24 forms, because two are always identical. – Appearing in the accompaniment of the theme at the beginning is the retrograde. The melody of the first variation is a transposition of the row beginning from C. The accompaniment is a double canon. Greater coherence is not pos-

sible. Not even the Netherlanders [composers of the Franco-Flemish School] managed that.'[3] The first movement, headed 'calmly paced', is divided into three parts, reminiscent of the conventional sonata movement though this is the only reminiscence of bygone times – indeed, Webern consciously wanted to connect with and continue the tradition. The first part of the movement is repeated, as well as the second and third parts combined. The movement is not characterised by a Classical development, but by imitation and variation. With '... parallel running rows, from whose superposition the harmonies result, Regina Busch[4] described what is typical of the motivic design in Webern's *Symphonie*. Specialist investigations are to be referred to for analysing the compositional technique.[5] Extreme sonic fragmentation of the anyhow thin sound – thanks to the chamber-music scoring –, the fraying out, sophisticated dynamics and specially nuanced sonics define the movement: with flageolet (and hence rich overtone effects), mutes used in both strings and winds, mutes inserted (horn), solo/tutti directives, pizzicato/arco bowing, playing on the bridge (strings) applied. Formally, the canon has become an essential construction principle: so, for example, the double canon of the first part and the mirror canon of the following section.

The second movement, on the other hand, is laid out as a variation movement, with a theme ('Very quiet') and seven variations, each 11 bars long, symmetrically correlated to each other (I–VII, II–VI, III–V). Each is instrumentally, individually coloured: after a dense first variation with the strings' plucked and bowed playing style, winds and harp almost solely take over the next section. Then the apparatus – with differentiated dynamics – is split up and spread apart, thereupon segmented in a block-like manner: in an extremely quiet (fourth) variation, forming the centre of the second movement. This is followed by a lively, rhyth-

---

[2] Hartmut Krones, article, 'Webern', in: *Die Musik in Geschichte und Gegenwart*, 2. neubearb. Ausgabe, hg. v. Ludwig Finscher, Personenteil 17 (Kassel, Basel, etc.), 2007, col. 604.

[3] Quotation from ibid., col. 609.
[4] Quotation from ibid., col. 604.
[5] In particular, the publication by Wolfgang Martin Stroh (footnote 1).

mically-accented section scored for strings and harp. Analogous to the second, the sixth variation gives precedence to the brass section, before the tutti forte sound gradually dissolves, petering out in a coda and fading away in pianissimo. If, without paying attention to the complicated formal structure, we look only at the optically minimalistic score, the symphony conveys – with its extremely dispersed movement (without a "melodic" framework), with extreme intervals, dynamic breaks, split instrumentation, sonic sparseness – an impression of the radically new in this Webern work, which, though remaining without a successor, has decisively shaped the musical avant-garde.

The reviewers of the New York première certainly described not only the amusing audience responses, but differentiated also the music: Paul Rosenfeld mentioned the "little piece is unconventional in its form", comparing it with the outline of a Cézanne watercolour and praising it as "complete in itself, but excessively subtle".[6] on the other hand, Olin Downes of the *New York Times* did not have a good word for the symphony, which he titled "The ultimate significance of nothing" and called it "the perfect fruition of futility".[7] No less controversial were the reviews after the first European performance in Vienna. Webern paradigmatically realised in his *Symphonie*, Op. 21, the compositional principles of imitation and variation, using the Schoenberg twelve-tone and serial technique further developed by his pupils – in continuation of tradition, on the one hand, as a radical new beginning, on the other.

Wolfgang Birtel
Translation: Margit L. McCorkle

---

[6] *The New Republic*, New York, from 1 August 1930, vol. 61, 198/199 – Quoted from Wolfgang Martin Stroh (footnote 1), 44f.
[7] *New York Times* of 19 December 1929 – Quoted from Wolfgang Martin Stroh (footnote 1), 46f.

VORWORT

Eine Sinfonie aus der Feder von Anton Webern (1883–1945), dem Meister der kleinen und kleinsten, der aphoristischen Form? Hatte sich die Gattung doch seit ihrer Konstituierung in der Zeit der Wiener Klassik, insbesondere durch Haydn und Mozart, immer weiterentwickelt: nicht nur – beginnend mit Beethoven – von den Dimensionen her, sondern auch inhaltlich. Die romantische Sinfonie führte schließlich von Schubert über Brahms, von Bruckner, Berlioz, Sibelius oder Schostakowitsch, um nur wenige Vertreter zu nennen, zu den Monumentalwerken Gustav Mahlers: Er experimentierte mit Extremen und sprengte alle Konventionen, was Dauer, Orchesterbesetzung, thematische Anlage, Intensität, formale Struktur anging. Webern reduzierte dagegen in seinen Opera alle Parameter geradezu radikal: u.a. mit minimalistischen Besetzungen, kurzen Spieldauern, der Bevorzugung von Piano-Dynamik-Bereichen, durchsichtiger Struktur – und in der thematischen Anlage mit der Realisierung von Zwölfton- und Reihen-Technik der *Zweiten Wiener Schule* (mit Schönberg, Berg, Webern). Welch ein Kontrast: von Gustav Mahlers achtem sinfonischem Opus, dem fast anderthalb Stunden dauernden Koloss der *Sinfonie der Tausend*, zu Weberns kammermusikalisch besetzter, weniger als zehn Minuten dauernder *Symphonie* op. 21.

Die Jahre ab 1922 waren bei Anton Webern von einem Wechsel zwischen Erfolg und Misserfolg geprägt: als Komponist wie als Dirigent. Einher gingen immer wieder finanzielle Probleme: „Käme ich nur endlich in eine unabhängigere Lage: um nur meiner Arbeit mich widmen zu können! […] Was gibt es Selbstverständlicheres, als daß ein Komponist eben dazu da ist, um zu komponieren!"[1], wandte sich Webern an den Verleger Emil Hertzka von der Universal Edition Wien. Und sein eindringlicher Hilferuf hatte Erfolg: Der Verlag gewährte ihm ab 1926 eine monatliche Zuwendung, die später noch erhöht wurde. Im gleichen Jahr konnte er mit der Uraufführung seiner *Fünf Stücke für Orchester* op. 10 bei der *Internationalen Gesellschaft für Neue Musik* (IGNM) in Zürich einen Erfolg weit über die Landesgrenzen hinaus verbuchen, der seinen Namen (als Komponist) verbreitete – eine Anerkennung, die er sich mittlerweile als Dirigent schon errungen hatte. Als kreativer Geist fühlte er sich dagegen in der Heimat noch weitgehend unverstanden.

1927 komponierte Webern sein *Streichtrio* op. 20 – das erste instrumentale Werk nach knapp zehn Jahren vokaler Opera – und beschäftigte sich wohl schon mit der Idee einer Sinfonie. Diese schloss er dann auch im August 1928 ab: überschrieben – so die Stichvorlage für den Verlag – *Symphonie für Klarinette, Baßklarinette, 2 Hörner, Harfe, 1. u. 2. Geige, Bratsche und Violoncell, op. 21*, gewidmet „Meiner Tochter Christine", Weberns dritter, 1919 geborener Tochter. Zur bereits in der Zeitschrift *Anbruch* angekündigten Uraufführung unter Hermann Scherchen kam es jedoch nicht – warum ist unklar. Im Juni 1929 meldete sich die amerikanische *League of Composers* und gab einen Auftrag für ein kammermusikalisches Werk, zum Honorar von 350 Dollar. Man einigte sich auf die – bereits vollendete – *Symphonie*, die dann auch am 18. Dezember zur Uraufführung kam, von Tumulten begleitet, die jedoch eher musikpolitisch begründet waren. Schon wenig später, am 24. Februar 1930, dirigierte der Komponist das Werk in Wien, Otto Klemperer im darauffolgenden Jahr in Berlin, und im selben Jahr kam es beim Festival der IGNM in London zur Aufführung. Weberns Verlag, die Universal Edition Wien, druckte die Partitur schon 1929.

Ausgehend von spättonaler Harmonik in seinen Werken um 1899, zeigten sich zuneh-

---

[1] Zit. nach Wolfgang Martin Stroh: *Anton Webern. Symphonie op. 21* (= *Meisterwerke der Musik* 11), München 1975, S. 3. Er bietet die detailreichste Untersuchung der musikalischen Struktur dieses Werkes.

mend Tendenzen zu einer Ausweitung der Harmonik und Expressivität, aber auch zu ungewöhnlichen Farben, differenzierter Dynamik und Artikulation, verbunden mit strukturellen Fragen, in deren Zentrum Variations- und Permutationstechniken standen. Die Streichquartettkompositionen *Fünf Sätze* op. 5 (1909) und *Sechs Bagatellen* op. 9 (1911) waren entscheidende Stationen – Belege für die extreme Verknappung und, bei den *Bagatellen*, für den generellen Abschied des Schönberg-Schülers von der herkömmlichen Tonalität: Die Sätze sind nahezu komplett in der Technik des Lehrers, also in der „Komposition mit zwölf nur aufeinander bezogenen Tönen", geschrieben. Endgültig wird diese Hinwendung dann ab dem *Kinderstück* (1924, für Klavier, o. op.) und den *Drei Volkstexte[n]* op. 17 (1924, für Gesang und Kammerensemble). Durch Weberns Konstruktion der Reihen – mit Aufteilung in Gruppen von vor allem sechs Tönen und Verwendung alter kontrapunktischer Techniken (Umkehrung, Krebs, Krebs der Umkehrung) – entstand „ein besonders dichtes Gewebe von Beziehungen"[2] – Tonalität wurde eliminiert und der formale Zusammenhalt durch ein enges motivisches Geflecht ersetzt.

Wie das Trio op. 20 und das Quartett op. 22 war auch Opus 21 zunächst dreisätzig konzipiert. Doch entschied sich Webern nach ersten Skizzen zu einem dritten Satz, es – auch in der *Symphonie* – bei einer zweisätzigen Anlage zu belassen. Über die zugrundeliegende Reihe schreibt der Komponist selbst: „Die Reihe lautet: F-As-G-Fis-B-A/Es-E-C-Cis-D- . – Sie hat die Eigentümlichkeit, daß der zweite Teil der Krebs des ersten ist […] Es gibt also hier nur 24 Formen, weil immer je zwei identisch sind. – In der Begleitung des Themas erscheint zu Beginn der Krebs. Die erste Variation ist in der Melodie eine Transposition der Reihe von C aus. Die Begleitung ist ein Doppelkanon. – Mehr Zusammenhang ist nicht möglich. Das

haben auch die Niederländer nicht zusammengebracht".[3] Der erste Satz, „Ruhig schreitend" überschrieben, ist dreigeteilt, was an den herkömmlichen Sonatensatz erinnert, auch wenn dies die einzige Reminiszenz an die Form vergangener Zeit darstellt – Webern wollte ja durchaus bewusst an die Tradition anknüpfen, sie weiterführen. Der erste Teil des Satzes wird wiederholt, ebenso wie der zweite und dritte Teil gemeinsam. Nicht von klassischer Entwicklung ist der Satz geprägt, sondern von Imitation und Variation. Mit „… parallel laufende[n] Reihenzüge[n], aus deren Überlagerung die Zusammenklänge resultieren", beschrieb Regina Busch[4] das Typische der motivischen Gestaltung in Weberns *Symphonie*. Für die Analyse der Kompositionstechnik, der Reihengestaltung sei auf Spezialuntersuchungen verwiesen.[5] Extreme klangliche Aufspaltung des ohnehin – dank der kammermusikalischen Besetzung – dünnen Klanges, Zerfaserung, ausgeklügelte Dynamik und insbesondere klangliche Raffinesse bestimmen den Satz: mit Flageolett (und damit betont obertonreichen Effekten), Dämpfereinsatz bei Streichern wie Bläsern, Stopfen (Horn), Solo-/Tutti-Anweisungen, Pizzicato-/Arco-Einsatz, Spielen am Steg (Streichern). Formal ist der Kanon zu einem wesentlichen Konstruktionsprinzip geworden: so beispielsweise im Doppelkanon des ersten Teils und im Spiegelkanon des folgenden Abschnitts.

Der zweite Satz ist dagegen als Variationen-Satz angelegt: mit einem Thema („Sehr ruhig") und sieben, jeweils 11 Takte langen Variationen, die symmetrisch aufeinander bezogen sind (I–VII, II–VI, III–V). Jede ist instrumentatorisch individuell gefärbt: nach einer dichten ersten Variation mit Streichern in gezupfter und gestrichener Spielweise übernehmen Bläser und Harfe fast alleine den nächsten Abschnitt. Dann wird der Apparat – bei differenzierter Dynamik – aufgesplittet und gespreizt, sodann blockartig aufgeteilt: in einer äußerst ruhigen

[2] Hartmut Krones, Art. „Webern", in: *Die Musik in Geschichte und Gegenwart*, 2. neubearb. Ausgabe, hg. v. Ludwig Finscher, Personenteil 17, Kassel, Basel usw. 2007, Sp. 604.

[3] Zit. nach ebda., Sp. 609.
[4] Zit. nach ebda., Sp. 604.
[5] Insbesondere auf die Veröffentlichung von Wolfgang Martin Stroh (Fußnote 1).

(vierten) Variation, die das Zentrum des zweiten Satzes bildet. Es folgt ein mit Streichern plus Harfe gesetzter lebhafter, rhythmisch betonter Teil. Die sechste Variation lässt – analog zur zweiten – den Bläsern den Vortritt, ehe sich in der letzten der Forte-Tutti-Klang nach und nach auflöst, in einer Coda ausläuft und im Pianissimo verklingt. Schaut man – ohne auf die komplizierte, formale Struktur zu achten – nur auf das optisch Minimalistische der Partitur, vermittelt die *Symphonie* mit ihrem extrem aufgelockerten Satz (ohne „melodisches" Gerüst), mit extremen Intervallen, dynamischen Brüchen, aufgeteilter Instrumentation, klanglicher Kargheit einen Eindruck vom radikal Neuen dieses Webern-Werkes, das ohne Nachfolger geblieben ist, aber die musikalische Avantgarde entscheidend geprägt hat.

Schon die Rezensenten der New Yorker Uraufführung beschrieben nicht nur die amüsierten Reaktionen des Publikums, sondern widmeten sich auch differenziert der Musik: Paul Rosenfeld erwähnte die „ungewöhnliche Form", verglich sie mit den Umrissen eines Aquarells von Cézanne, lobte sie als „in sich vollkommen und zugleich unerhört kunstreich"[6]. Olin Downes von der *New York Times* fand dagegen kein gutes Wort für die *Symphonie*, der er den Titel „Die letzte Bedeutung von Nichts" gab und über die er von einer „allzu dürftigen Musik"[7] sprach. Nicht minder kontrovers waren die Besprechungen nach der ersten europäischen Aufführung in Wien. Webern hat in seiner *Symphonie* op. 21 die Kompositionsprinzipien von Imitation und Variation, unter Verwendung der Schönbergschen Zwölfton- und der durch den Schüler weiterentwickelten Reihentechnik, paradigmatisch realisiert – in Fortführung der Tradition einerseits, als radikaler Neuanfang andererseits.

Wolfgang Birtel

---

[6] *The New Republic*, New York, vom 8.1.1930, Vol. 61, S. 198/199 – zit. und übersetzt von Wolfgang Martin Stroh (s. Fußnote 1), S. 44f.
[7] *New York Times* vom 19.12.1929 – zit. und übersetzt von Wolfgang Martin Stroh (s. Fußnote 1), S. 46f.

SYMPHONY

Meiner Tochter Christina

Anton Webern
(1883–1945)
Op. 21

I

2

II
VARIATIONEN

III. VARIATION

VI. VARIATION

VII. VARIATION

etwas breiter   rit. _ _ _ _ tempo   rit. _ _ _ _ tempo rit. _ _ _